MILNER CRAFT SERIES

Embroidery
A beginner's Workshop

MILNER CRAFT SERIES

Embroidery
A beginner's Workshop

Jock Levinson

SALLY MILNER PUBLISHING

First published in 1992 by
Sally Milner Publishing Pty Ltd
67 Glassop Street
Birchgrove NSW 2041 Australia

© Jock Levinson, 1992

Production by Sylvana Scannapiego,
Island Graphics
Cover design and colour layout
by Kate Golightly
Layout by Valda Brook
Illustrations by Anna Warren
Photography by Andre Martin
Typeset in Australia by Asset Typesetting Pty Ltd
Printed in Australia by Impact Printing

National Library of Australia
Cataloguing-in-Publication data:

Levinson, Jock.
    Embroidery, a beginner's workshop

    Includes index.
    ISBN 1 86351 086 9.

    1. Embroidery. I. Title. (Series: Milner craft series).

746.44

FOREWORD

by
LADY DUNSTAN

To the beginner, instructional books can be frustratingly incomprehensible. Experts have difficulty understanding that matters which are elementary to them can be a mystery to others just starting. This book is different; the author is an expert in teaching beginners. From long experience she knows their problems and how to solve them.

I have been associated with the Embroiderers' Guild of South Australia Incorporated for a number of years. It has been a rewarding experience. I have opened their exhibitions and visited their Club Rooms many times. I have shared with other South Australians a great pride in their work; highlights have been their contribution to the new Parliament House in Canberra and the new Law Courts in Adelaide.

This book is based on sound principles. It will help to make embroidery a satisfying challenge for many people, bringing much pleasure and fulfilment.

We owe a great debt of gratitude to 'Jock' Levinson for this important contribution.

DEDICATION

Working with the teachers and students of the
Embroiderers' Guild of South Australia during the past
eight years has proved that this set of projects 'works'.
I would like to thank them, together with friends
and my family for making this book possible.

'Jock' Levinson

CONTENTS

GUIDE TO STITCH INSTRUCTIONS

GENERAL RULES

TO BEGIN THE EMBROIDERY

There are two methods used in this book.

1. Sew a small back stitch at the edge of the material where the line of embroidery starts.
   Put the needle in at A. Bring it up at B.
   Repeat this once, then begin the embroidery stitches.

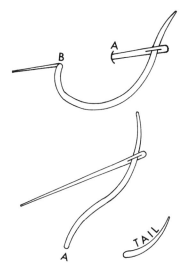

2. Start with a tail. Thread the needle and put it into the material about 2 cm (¾") away from where you wish to start the embroidery.
   Leave the tail about 4 cm (1½") long so that it can be threaded into the needle later. Bring the needle up where you wish to start the embroidery. Later, take the tail to the 'wrong' side of your work. Thread the tail into the needle. Take the needle under three or four stitches — not into the material. Cut off excess thread.

TO FINISH OFF EMBROIDERY

Take the thread through to the 'back' or 'wrong' side. Take the needle under three or four stitches — not into the material. Cut off remaining thread.

As you specialise in other techniques, you will find other ways of beginning and ending.

LENGTH OF THREAD

A piece of thread 45 cm (18") long is generally used.

STIFFENING

Instead of Pergosel, you can use plastic from an ice-cream or margarine container.

TRACING THE DESIGN

Use tracing paper or greaseproof paper. Do not use waxed paper.

PRESSING

Dampen the material with water. Place on soft padded surface with the 'wrong' side uppermost. Put iron onto material — lift up — don't move the iron back and forth, or you will stretch the material in some places.

AIDA MATERIAL MAT

MATERIALS REQUIRED

- Aida cloth 15 cm x 15 cm (6″ x 6″)
- DMC cotton perle thread No. 8: two colours for running stitch and some to match the material colour
- Tapestry needle size 24 (these needles are blunt and are used when sewing between threads of the material)

METHOD

Thread the needle. As a guide you will need approximately 45 cm (18″) of thread.

Start the running stitch: Count 20 'holes' along one edge of the material, mark with a pin.

On the row of holes you have marked, start the 'running stitch' by putting the needle down into the second hole from the right-hand edge. Take the needle up at the fourth hole and continue in this way across the material. Be careful not to pull the end of the thread past the edge of the material. Sew across the second, third and fourth sides by counting in the same way.

With the second colour, sew another row of running stitch next to the first row but two rows of holes away towards the inside of the material. For this row of stitches, put the needle into the second hole from the edge, from below, and down at the fourth.
Complete all four sides like this:

For the edge of the material embroider a row of 'cross stitch' around all four sides.

Count 12 holes from the edge of the material beside the running stitches, mark with a pin. Thread the needle with thread to match the material, approximately 45 cm (18″) long. Put the needle in at A, leaving a tail long enough to thread into the needle later. Bring the needle up at B (the hole you marked with your pin). Count two holes along the same row of holes, two holes up, and put the needle in at C. The needle comes out again at D which is straight down from C and in line with B. Continue these slanted stitches.

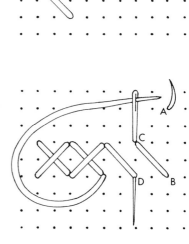

When you get near to the corner, you need to count so that the last cross stitch in this row is the same distance from the running stitch (eight holes) when you start the second side. As you reach a corner you need to turn the material around, so that you keep the slanting stitches slanting the same way. When all four sides are completed, continue using the same holes but cross each stitch all around.

Finish the cross stitch like this: After the last cross stitch is complete, the needle should be on the back or wrong side of the material. Thread it under at least three stitches, not into the material, and cut off the excess. Bring the tail to the wrong side and thread it into the needle and under at least three stitches, and cut off the excess. If you need to join the thread on the way along use this same method.

The embroidery is now complete, fray the threads on all sides back to the cross stitch. The cross-stitched edge will prevent any further fraying.

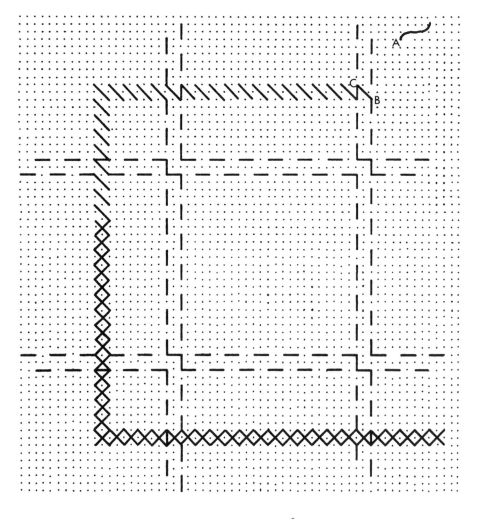

CHECKED GINGHAM BAG

MATERIALS REQUIRED

- Checked Gingham approximately 30 cm x 30 cm (12" x 12")
- Tape for a drawstring
- DMC cotton perle thread No. 5, white
- Crewel needle size 6

METHOD

Fold the material in half. The two long sides become the sides of the bag. Decide which one of the short sides is to be the bottom of the bag. Measure 8 cm (3") from the bottom of the bag, and mark the spot with a pin. Thread the needle with 45 cm (18") of thread, and take a small stitch at the spot marked with the pin. Sew through the same holes once again to make an anchor for the end of the thread. This stitch is called a 'back stitch'.

The picture will show that in this article the stitches are only over the pale red or blue squares not the dark ones. Embroider three rows of cross stitch across the bag, leaving a row of squares between each two rows.

INTERLACING

No stitches in the interlacing technique go into the material. Thread the needle with approx 45 cm (18") of white cotton. Anchor the thread with a back stitch and weave the thread in and out of the crosses, making a pattern.

Make up the bag by machine so that it is ready for you to thread a tape in the top as a drawstring.

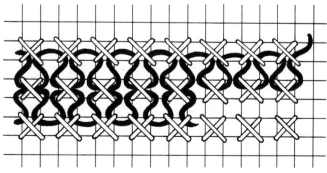

ROSEBUD BAG

MATERIALS REQUIRED

- Aida cloth, cream, approximately 30 cm x 30 cm (12″ x 12″)
- Tape for a drawstring
- DMC stranded cotton thread: green 502, pink 309, and pink 899
- Tapestry needle size 24

METHOD

Using two strands of green thread make a small back stitch, to anchor the thread, 7 cm (3″) from bottom edge of bag. Embroider a row of cross stitches across the material, making a stitch and leaving space for a stitch, right across the fabric. Fill in the spaces you have left with cross stitches in pale pink.

Leave eight squares above this row and repeat the above two-coloured row. Count 11 squares above this second row and repeat the two bands of two-coloured rows (see photograph).

ROSEBUDS

These are embroidered in lazy daisy stitch. Take two strands of darker pink thread, anchor the thread with a back stitch two squares below the top row of the cross stitches. Bring the needle up eight squares from the left-hand edge of the material. This is A. Hold the thread to the left with your thumb, put the needle down into the same hole and bring the needle out at B, two squares down over the loop of thread. Pull the thread firmly to make a well-shaped loop. Now put the needle in again at B and hold the loop in place. Bring the thread out four squares to the right, on the same line as A. Complete the row in this way.

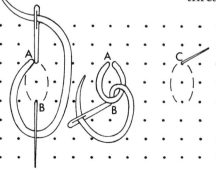

Take two strands of paler pink thread and embroider another lazy daisy stitch around the first one. Finish the row.

The stalk is embroidered in fly stitch, which is just like lazy daisy with its arms apart. Bring the needle up one square to the left of A and put it in one square to the right of A. Bring the needle out at B and complete the stalk by putting it in two holes down. Continue along the row. Repeat this row, making stalks on the other rows of rosebud cross stitches.

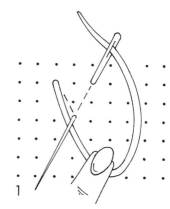

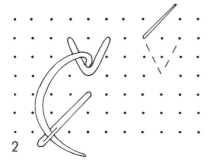

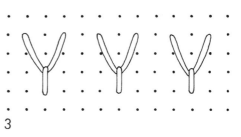

YOUR NAME IN BACK STITCH

In the wider space between the two rows of pattern, you may like to put your name. Follow the chart on this page, drawing the letters of your name onto graph or squared paper. Leave one clear space between each two letters.

Start with two strands of darker pink thread and embroider in back stitch, keeping the back as neat as you can. Work over one square for each stitch.

BACK STITCH

Bring the needle out one square to the left of the line you wish to make. Put it in one square to the right (where you want the line to start). Bring the needle out again one square to the left of the stitch A and back up again to B.

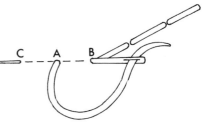

Make up the bag by machine. Thread a tape in the top as a drawstring.

PROJECT 4

JAM-JAR COVER

These covers, when finished, look like little shower caps.

MATERIALS REQUIRED

- Unbleached calico or other cotton fabric approximately 15 cm x 15 cm (6″ x 6″)
- Round hat elastic
- DMC stranded cotton thread in the colour of the fruit you choose to embroider, and green for the leaves
- White sewing-machine thread
- Bias binding, optional
- Crewel needle size 6

METHOD

Trace the design of the fruit you want to embroider onto a piece of greaseproof paper. Simply put the paper over the picture and draw over the design with a pencil. Find the centre of the material by folding it in half one way, making a crease, then folding it the other way. The centre is the point at which the creases intersect. Pin the traced design over the centre. Slide a piece of dressmaker's carbon between the cloth and the design. Use a sharp pencil and go over the design firmly. Embroider the fruit in chain stitches and the leaves in chain stitch and back stitch (see photograph).

CHAIN STITCH

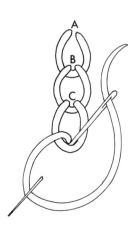

Start with a tail. Bring the needle up at the starting point A. Put your left thumb onto the thread. Put the needle in again at A and bring it out at B (2½ mm — ¹⁄₁₀″ further on). Hold the thread over the loop with your thumb. Put the needle in at B and out at C. Continue this way.

BACK STITCH

Start with a tail. Bring the needle up at A. Take it down back to B (2 mm — $\frac{1}{10}$" to the right of A). Bring the needle up at C and take it back to A.

When the embroidery is completed: Turn the material onto the wrong side and, using a saucer as a guide, draw a circle with a pencil. You make like to finish around the edges with bias binding or just follow the line with a machine stitch, sewing two rows very close together. Cut around this line, 1 mm ($\frac{1}{20}$") outside the line of stitching. The material may fray a little, but only up to the machine stitching.

Draw a pencil line 2 cm ($\frac{3}{4}$") inside the first line. Use a zig-zag stitch on the sewing machine to oversew round hat elastic. Leave enough elastic at the beginning and end of the circle to draw up and tie into a knot. Trim excess elastic.

SMALL TISSUE-PACK COVER

MATERIALS REQUIRED

- A piece of plain coloured linen (tea towel or dress material) 27 cm x 16 cm (11″ x 6½″)
- DMC stranded cotton thread:
    colour of your choice for flowers
    yellow for centre of flowers
    green for leaves
- Crewel needle size 8

METHOD

Cut the material following the grain. This will ensure that all corners are right angles and the material will lie correctly when folded. You will need to draw out a thread of the material along each side and cut along this line. To do this, measure each side, mark with a pin, withdraw thread. Cut along these lines left in the material.

Dampen the material with water and iron it. Fold it exactly in half so that the two shorter sides are together. Press with iron. This is the middle fold. Measure 9 cm (3½″) from this fold on one side. Mark with a pin. Fold and press towards centre. Repeat on other side of middle fold. Bring these two folded lines to the middle. Make sure they are exactly together. Press with iron.

Trace the design in the diagram onto tracing or greaseproof paper using a sharp pencil. Place the line marked 'fold' on the drawing along the middle folds of the material. Pin in place. Slip dressmaker's carbon paper between the material and the pencil design. Draw

CENTRE FOLDS

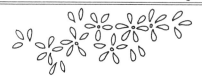

over the design carefully. Press very firmly with a sharply pointed pencil. You will find it easier to make one line for each petal. Lift the carbon paper away, not the tracing, and make sure the design is clear before you unpin the tracing paper.

Thread the needle with two strands of cotton thread for the flowers. Start with a tail. Embroider the flowers and leaves in small lazy daisy stitches. For the yellow centres of the flowers work a back stitch, then work another one on top of the first one.

TO MAKE UP

Turn the material onto the wrong side. Do not undo the folds nearest the embroidery. See that these two folds are close together. Stitch by machine across each end 1 cm (½″) from the end. Turn onto right side. Press with iron. Tuck a packet of tissues into the cover.

NAME BADGE

MATERIALS REQUIRED

- Aida cloth approximately 15 cm x 7 cm (6" x 3")
- Stiffening — Pergasel 2 cm x 15 cm (1" x 6")
- DMC stranded cotton thread:
    black on pale background material
    white on dark background material
- Sewing-machine thread same colour as material
- A small safety-pin to secure badge to your clothes
- Tapestry needle size 24
- Crewel needle size 8

METHOD

As in Project 3, select the letters of your name and make your own chart. Count the squares in the chart to find the middle of your name. Mark that point. Count the squares in the material to find the middle and mark with a pin. Start to embroider your name, working from the middle of the chart and the middle of the material.

Thread the needle with two strands of thread (using tapestry needle). Work in back stitch over one square.

When the embroidery is completed cut the Pergasel 2 cm (1") longer than the embroidered name. This makes the badge 1 cm (½") longer at each end than the embroidery. Remove the paper from the back of the Pergasel and place the stiffening evenly onto the back of the embroidered material. Make sure it is straight. First fold the ends of the material over the stiffening, then fold one of the long sides. Pin this firmly and tightly. Trim excess material. Finally pin the second long side. To hold this all in place use herringbone stitch because it will extend along and over the raw edge of the material and keep it as flat as possible.

HERRINGBONE STITCH

Thread the needle with machine cotton (crewel needle). Work from left to right over an imaginary double line.

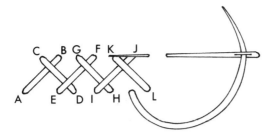

The top row of stitches is worked 1 cm (½″) above the raw edge of the material. The bottom line of stitches is worked just below the raw edge of the material.

Anchor the thread with a small backstitch at the bottom left hand end. This is A. Put the needle in 1 cm (½″) above and 1 cm (½″) to the right of A. This is B. Bring the needle up 2 mm (¹⁄₁₀″) to the left of B at C. Put the needle in 1 cm (½″) to the right of A. Continue across the badge, adding extra stitches if necessary to make a neat, secure finish.

Sew a safety-pin onto the back of the badge using machine thread. The badge is now ready to wear.

EMBROIDERING BUTTERFLIES ON A T-SHIRT

MATERIALS REQUIRED

- T-shirt
- Waste canvas 12 mesh 10 cm (4″)
- DMC stranded cotton thread: two bright colours for the butterfly, plus black for the body
- Crewel needle size 6

METHOD

The canvas is woven with two threads close together. These are counted as one. This is the way of getting pleasing, even cross stitches when embroidering on material that is not of an even weave. Cut a piece of canvas 44 threads x 28 threads. Tack the piece of canvas onto the T-shirt, being careful not to stretch the T-shirt material. Start the tail of the butterfly (with a tail) three threads from the bottom of the canvas. Taking three strands of black thread, proceed to cross stitch the body over two threads. The feelers are worked in back stitch. As you can see in the chart, the wings nearest the head are embroidered in one colour and the other in the paler of the colours you have chosen.

When the embroidery is complete, carefully cut the canvas away after removing the tacking thread. Wet the canvas and pull the threads of the canvas from under the cross stitches. Embroider as many additional butterflies as you wish.

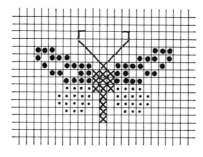

PROJECT 1: AIDA MATERIAL MAT

PROJECT 2: GINGHAM BAG

PROJECT 3: ROSEBUD BAG

PROJECT 4: JAM-JAR COVER

PROJECT 5: SMALL TISSUE-PACK COVER

PROJECT 6: NAME BADGE

PROJECT 7: EMBROIDERED BUTTERFLIES ON T-SHIRT

PROJECT 8: PULLED FABRIC EXERCISE; AND PROJECT 9: PULLED FABRIC MAT

PROJECT 10: PATCHWORK FLOWER FOR DECORATION

PROJECT 11: CROSS-STITCH PICTURE AND ALTERNATIVE PROJECT 11: CANVAS-WORK PICTURE

PROJECT 12: COLOURED LINEN MAT

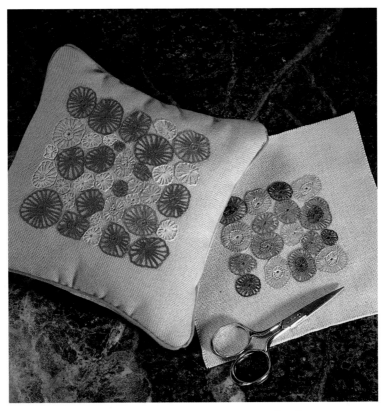

PROJECT 13: BROOCH CUSHION OR LARGE PIN CUSHION

PROJECT 14: MANY STITCHES BAG

OBJECTS FOR CHATELAINE (CLOCKWISE FROM TOP): PROJECT 19: STRAP; PROJECT 16: SCISSORS CASE; PROJECT 18: NEEDLE CASE; PROJECT 15: PIN CUSHION; AND PROJECT 17: THIMBLE BAG

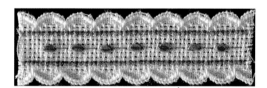

DETAIL OF EMBROIDERY FOR STRAP OF CHATELAINE

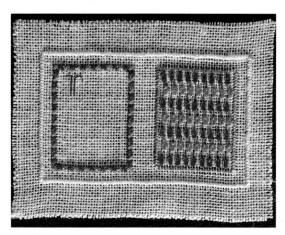

DETAIL OF EMBROIDERY FOR NEEDLE CASE

DETAIL OF EMBROIDERY FOR PIN CUSHION

PROJECT 20: WHITE LINEN MAT

DETAIL OF STITCHING FOR WHITE LINEN MAT

PULLED FABRIC EXERCISE

MATERIALS REQUIRED

- A piece of even-weave linen, not too closely woven, 15 cm x 15 cm (6″ x 6″)
- DMC cotton perle thread No. 12
- Tapestry needle size 24 or 26

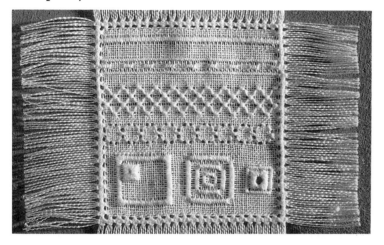

METHOD

This embroidery makes different lacy patterns by pulling the threads of the material together in even groups.

Row one: Start 3 cm (1″) from the top of the material and 3 cm (1″) from the left side.

Leave a tail on the right side of the linen. Work in satin stitch over four threads at a time, as in the first diagram. Finish 3 cm (1″) from the right edge. Pull each stitch firmly. Put the needle under the last three or four stitches, on the back of the embroidery — not into the material — pull through. Cut off excess thread. Treat the tail in the same way.

Row two: Start six threads below the first row.

Embroider in satin stitch over two threads. Complete row as before.

Row three: Start this row four threads below the last row.

Work six satin stitches over four threads. Leave six spaces, work six satin stitches. Complete the row in this way, pulling the thread firmly.

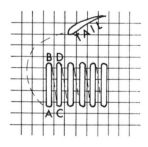

Row four: This is another row of satin stitches over two threads.

The last three rows make a very attractive border pattern.

WAVE STITCH

This is the next pattern on the sampler. Work from right to left. Leave a tail. Bring the needle up at A, take it down two threads to the right and four above at B. Bring the needle out four threads to the left (in line with B) at C. Put it in at A. Bring the needle out four threads to the left (in line with A) at D. Put it in at C. Follow across the material in this way. If repeat rows of this stitch are embroidered, a lacy pattern is formed.

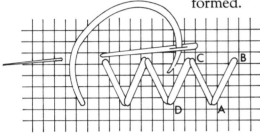

RINGED BACK STITCH

This is worked from right to left. Leave a tail. Bring the needle up at A and down at B, three threads down from A. Bring needle up at C, three threads further on than A and three to the left of A. The needle goes down at A. Next bring the needle up three threads to the left of C, at D, and down at C. The fourth stitch brings the needle up at E, four threads down and four to the left of D, and down at D. Bring the needle up four threads down at F and down at E.

Follow the diagram in this way across the material and then turn the material around and complete each 'ring' on the way back. If repeat rows of this stitch are embroidered, a lacy pattern is formed.

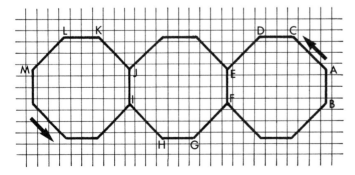

Square designs worked in satin stitch and eye stitch are next on the sampler. See the photograph for some of the variations you can do. The first pattern is a square of satin stitch over four threads with a square of eye stitch in the top left-hand corner. The second pattern is a square of satin stitch with two smaller squares of satin stitch inside. The third pattern is a square of satin stitch over two threads with a square of eye stitch inside it.

EYE STITCH

This stitch consists of satin stitches *all* taken into the same hole in the centre of a square. Work each stitch over four threads, leaving one thread between stitches. Work nine stitches on each side of the square. Finish each 'eye' by threading the needle under three or four stitches (not into the fabric), on the wrong side. Treat the tail in the same way.

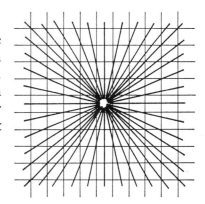

FOUR-SIDED OR SQUARE STITCH

Complete the sampler by working an edge in square or four-sided stitch. Work from right to left. Start six threads above the first row of satin stitch, leaving a tail. Bring the needle up at A. Put it in four threads up at B. Bring it out at C, four threads to the left and four down. Put the needle in at A and out four threads to the left of B at D. Put needle in at B and out four threads to the left of A at C. Pull all stitches firmly. This row of stitches around the decorated area makes a strong border. Fray the threads of the sampler to this line of stitches.

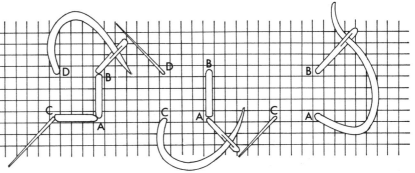

PULLED FABRIC MAT

MATERIALS REQUIRED

- A square piece of even-weave linen 15 cm x 15 cm (6″ x 6″)
- DMC cotton perle thread No. 12 to match the linen
- Machine sewing cotton for tacking
- Tapestry needle size 24 or 26

METHOD

Thread the needle with tacking thread. Find the middle of one side by counting the threads. Mark with a pin. Anchor the thread on this line and follow the weave across the material in tacking stitch. Repeat this on the second side, dividing the linen into four.

Thread the needle with DMC cotton perle thread. Start with a tail. When using counted thread stitches, start in the middle of one side. Start 3 cm (1″) from the edge of the mat with square stitches and work over four threads. When only 3 cm (1″) remains in that row, turn and continue in square stitches along the second side. Make sure the mat is square by embroidering the same number of stitches along each side. Complete all four sides.

Decorate the mat with a leaf shape, filling the leaf shape with wave stitch and using chain stitch around the shape to complete the embroidery. Alternatively, decorate the mat with squares of satin stitch as in chart. You may like to put an eye stitch in the centre of each square. Fray the four edges of the mat. Dampen with water and iron on the wrong side.

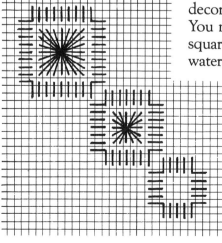

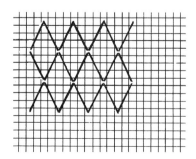

PATCHWORK FLOWER FOR DECORATION

MATERIALS REQUIRED

- Pretty floral cotton material. Each of the seven hexagon patches needs about 8 cm x 8 cm (3″ x 3″)
- You may like the central patch made in a plain fabric to form the centre of the flower
- Machine sewing thread No. 50 to match the colour of the patches
- Crewel needle size 9 or 10
- Two hexagon templates. Available in shops or can be accurately transferred from the pictures shown here onto very firm paper

METHOD

Cut out one of the large templates from stiff paper. Place it on the material, making sure that one of the straight sides follows exactly the grain of the material (that is, one of the threads woven across the fabric). This is very important. Pin in place and carefully cut around the template. Cut six floral pieces and one plain in this way.

Cut seven firm paper templates in the small size. Put one of the small paper templates against the wrong side of the material patch you have ready. See that one edge of the paper follows the straight grain of the material, and that an even amount of material is showing all around the template. Pin carefully with two pins so that the material does not move out of place.

Thread the needle with thread about 45 cm (18″) long. Fold the material over the paper and tack the two together. Turn the next side down and tack, making sure that the turn over follows the exact shape of the paper template. The patches will fit together very easily if you are neat with the turnings. Complete all six sides and all seven patches in this way. Assemble the hexagons, the six floral ones around the plain one.

Thread the needle with about 45 cm (18″) coloured thread to match the patches. Arrange the patches so that the grain of the material is running the same way as a whole piece of material would do. Put two patches together back to back, wrong sides outside. Sew the two patches together along one straight side, using top stitch.

TOP STITCHING

Top stitching is worked by putting the needle straight across, through both patches. Sew close to the edge, and anchor the thread well. Continue with these straight stitches about 1.5 mm (¹⁄₁₀″) apart. Sew over the last stitch twice and finish with a back stitch through the material only. Flatten the two patches out and put them in place so that you can see which are the next two sides to sew together. When the patchwork 'flower' is complete, remove the tacking and the templates. The flower is now ready to sew as a decoration onto a skirt or bag. There are many interesting ways to use the flower you have made. A great many of them sewn together make a patchwork quilt.

CROSS-STITCH PICTURE

MATERIALS REQUIRED

- Even-weave linen, pale green, 12 cm x 9 cm (5″ x 3½″)
- Tapestry needle size 24 or 26
- DMC stranded cotton thread: white, pink 309, pale yellow 727, dark green 3362, green 522

The small English daisies are embroidered in white, using two strands of thread. The pink edge to the flowers is worked in back stitch with one strand of thread. The stalks are also worked in back stitch in dark green, using two strands of thread.

METHOD

Thread the needle with machine cotton thread. Find the middle of one side by counting the threads across the linen. Mark with a pin. Tack a line across this mark. Repeat this for the second side. This will divide the material into four. Where the tacking crosses is the centre of the material. The chart has arrows marking the mid-lines on each side. These lines help you to put the stitches in the correct place, as you will be counting from the line to where the stitching has to be. Follow the chart and the list which tells you which colour to use in each square.

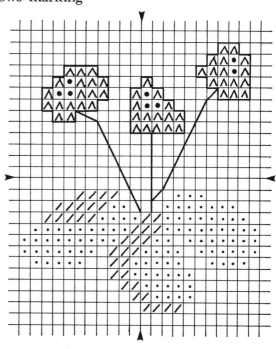

/	3362	Dark green
·	522	Green
∧		White
•	727	Pale yellow
−	309	Pink

− − Back stitch around white flowers

When the embroidery has been completed, put it into a pretty frame.

CANVAS-WORK PICTURE

MATERIALS REQUIRED

- A piece of single-thread canvas, 12 threads to 2.5 cm (1"), 15 cm x 15 cm (6" x 6")
- DMC tapestry wool, one skein of each: white, yellow 727, green 7376, green 7377, background blue 7593 or pink 7193
- Tapestry needle size 22
- Small embroidery frame

METHOD

Find the centre line of the canvas (each way) by counting. Mark with pins and tack lines with machine cotton. The chart you will follow is marked in the same way.

Put the canvas into the embroidery frame by putting the outer ring of the frame onto the table. Next put the canvas over the frame. Now put the smaller or inner circle of the frame over the canvas and push it down into the larger circle. Turn the framed canvas over onto the right side.

Thread the needle with white wool. To decide where to start, look at the list at the bottom of the chart. It will show a different symbol for each colour. The symbol for white is a cross. Find a cross on the chart near to where the centre lines cross. You will find it necessary to count from these lines many times as you progress.

TENT STITCH

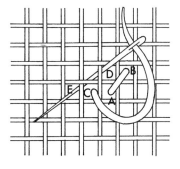

Tent stitch is the stitch used. Start with a tail. Bring the needle up at A. Put the needle in one thread to the right and one thread above at B. Bring the needle up one thread to the left of A at C, and down one thread to the left of B at D.

When the flowers and leaves have been completed, fill in the background with blue or pink. At this stage you have to decide what size and shape the frame for the picture will be. The background must cover the canvas generously, to leave no canvas showing when the embroidery is framed.

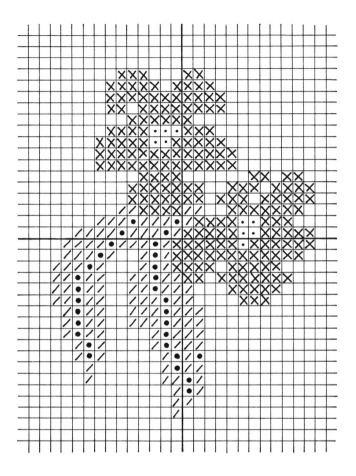

✕	White	
·	Yellow	727
╱	Green	7376
●	Green	7377
	Blue	7539
	Pink	7193

COLOURED LINEN MAT

MATERIALS REQUIRED

- A piece of plain coloured linen (tea towel or dress material) approximately 15 cm x 15 cm (6″ x 6″)
- DMC stranded cotton thread in the same colour as the material
- Crewel needle size 10

METHOD

Draw two threads from one side of the material 3 cm (1″) from the edge. Repeat along the other three sides.

Hem stitch will hold the frayed edge of the mat just as the cross stitch and square stitch have done. Thread the needle with two strands of thread. As usual, start with a tail.

HEM STITCH

Work from left to right on the inner side of the withdrawn threads. Start away from a corner, with a tail. Bring the needle up two threads below the withdrawn threads. Put the needle in three threads to the right and pick up these threads. Pull the needle through and hold the thread with your thumb. Put the needle into the gap made, from the back. Bring it up two threads directly below. Continue in this way around all four sides. When all embroidery has been completed, fray the edges to the hemstitching.

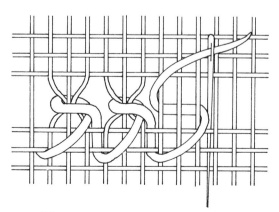

TO DECORATE THE MAT

Choose a small design you like or use the design in this book. Trace the design as explained in Project 4. Transfer the design onto the mats as in Project 4. Place the design in a corner of the mat so that when a vase is placed on it, the embroidery can still be seen.

Thread the needle with two strands of thread. Leave a tail. Follow the lines of the design with the stitches. Embroider the leaves in back stitch, or lazy daisy stitch, keeping the stitches small (2 mm/$\frac{1}{10}$" in length). The flowers or birds are embroidered in chain stitch (2 mm/$\frac{1}{10}$" in length). The stems are embroidered in stem stitch.

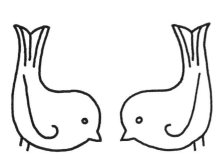

STEM STITCH

Start with a tail and work left to right. Bring the needle up on a line at A. Take the needle down 3 mm ($\frac{1}{8}$") further along the line at B. Bring the needle up midway between A and B at C. Take the needle down 3 mm ($\frac{1}{8}$") to the right at D. Bring the needle up at B. Take it down again at E, 3 mm ($\frac{1}{8}$") to the right. Continue to follow the line in this way.

When all the embroidery has been completed, fray the edges up to the hem stitching. Damp the fabric and iron on the wrong side.

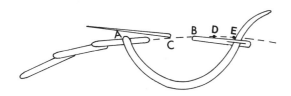

BROOCH CUSHION OR LARGE PIN CUSHION

MATERIALS REQUIRED

- Two pieces of firm material, not too thin or tightly woven, 15 cm x 15 cm (6″ x 6″)
- DMC stranded cotton thread. It is interesting to use four shades of the colour of the material. If you have pink material, choose different-coloured pinks, both dark and light
- Crewel needle size 9
- Filling for the cushion

METHOD

Find the centre of one piece of the material. This will be the top of the cushion. Trace the design from the book onto greaseproof paper. Pin to the centre of the material, down two sides of the paper. Slip a piece of dressmaker's carbon paper between paper and cloth. Press very firmly with a sharp pencil so the design shows clearly on the fabric.

The 'flowers' are embroidered in button-hole stitch using six strands of thread. Put the needle into the material, leaving a tail to be woven into the back of the stitches later. Bring the needle up at A. Hold the thread with your left thumb, as you did with chain stitch. Bring the needle out at B over the thread. Put the needle in at C. Hold the thread with your left thumb. Bring the needle out at D. Continue, following the lines of the design. Where there are two circles of stitches, embroider the outer one first, then the inner one.

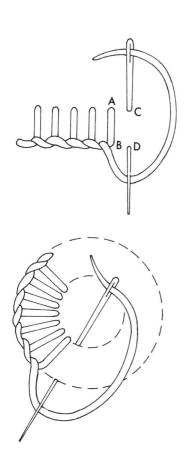

When the embroidery has been completed, pin the two pieces of material together with wrong sides outside. You may decide to sew these together by machine or you can follow a line marked in back stitch, using machine cotton to match the material. Remember to leave an opening in the middle of one side. You need to turn the cushion on to the right side and fill it with wool stuffing. Pin the two sides of the opening neatly together. Sew the opening together using small nearly invisible stitches.

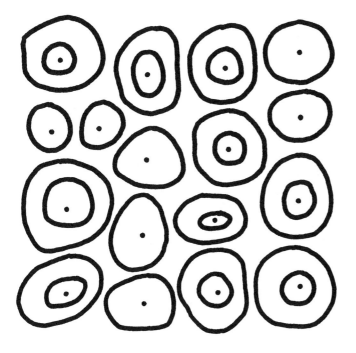

MANY STITCHES BAG

MATERIALS REQUIRED

- Floba, a coarse, even-weave fabric, natural colour, 46 x 26 cm (18½″ x 10″)
- If you wish to put a circular bottom on the bag, a piece 17 x 17 cm (7″ x 7″) is also needed
- A piece of material for the handle, 32 x 9 cm (11″ x 4″)
- Lining, figured or plain, to echo the colours in the embroidery, 46 x 22 cm (18½″ x 9″)
- Some thick Dacron wadding will be sufficient to stiffen the bottom, 17 x 17 cm (7″ x 7″)
- DMC stranded threads: Three browns — 3371, 830, 840. Three greens — 3011, 3012, 3013. Three rose-pinks — 221, 223, 224, or three apricot pinks — 352, 758, 3328, or three blues — 930, 931, 932. One yellow — 676

  Start with one skein of each of these 10 skeins. Some colours are used more than others. Buy others as needed.

- Machine sewing thread in a natural colour for finishing bag by machine
- Tapestry needle size 22 or 24

METHOD

By the time you start this project, you will have practised most of the stitches on this bag in other projects. It is now a matter of grouping stitches together to form pleasing patterns.

By starting 6 cm (2½″) from the base of the bag with the darkest colour and the heaviest stitches, we follow the rules of design. Gradually, the lighter colours and the less dense patterns are brought in. Follow the chart showing the colour used and the stitches. The picture will show the count of threads and spacing of the stitches. It is suggested that about 4-6 cm (1½-2½″) of each line be worked so that a pattern is established. The rest of the embroidery can then be done without referring to the chart.

1. Start the first line of embroidery 6 cm (2½″) from base of bag on the long side of the material. Using darkest-brown thread, satin stitch over two, three, four and five threads, then decrease over four, three and two threads. Continue to end of row.

2. Turn the material around and work the same way to blend with the first row. Work this row in darkest pink, apricot or blue.

3. Leave five threads, chain stitch over two threads in darkest green.

4. Leave four threads, button-hole over two, three, four and five threads, decreasing over four, three, two, in dark-brown. Leave two threads between stitches.

5. Be careful in the count here. Turn work around and work in button-hole as above. The smallest stitch starts nine threads away from previous row. The stitches blend well to leave diamond shapes. Work this row in dark pink, apricot or blue.

6. In dark green thread, fill in the diamonds in satin stitch.

7. Leave six threads. Work in satin stitch over three threads in mid-brown thread.

8/9. With mid-pink, apricot or blue, back stitch over two threads on each side of row 9.

10. Leave four threads, stem stitch over four threads in mid-green thread.

11. Leave one thread and using mid-brown thread, herringbone stitch over seven threads. Pick up two threads — leave two threads top and bottom.

12. Following the same lines, work in herringbone stitch in mid-pink, apricot or blue. Pick up the two threads left by previous row of stitches — top and bottom.

13. Leave one thread. Stem stitch in mid-green as at row 12.

14. Leave five threads. Cross stitch over two threads with mid-green thread.

15/16. Work these two lines together. Leave four threads. Cross stitch over two threads three times. Now — in the line above sew one cross stitch above the middle cross stitch. Repeat all along the line.

17. Using mid-pink, apricot or blue thread, work four cross stitches as in illustration. These form little flowers.

18. Fill the centre of each flower with a cross stitch in mid-brown.

19. Leave four threads above the top cross stitch, and work three rows of running stitch (over two threads under two threads), leaving one thread between rows.

20. Leave seven threads. Work in lazy daisy stitch over three threads in mid-pink, apricot or blue. Leave 10 threads and repeat along row.

21. Fly stitch in pale green, one thread each side of lazy daisy and taking the stalk down over five threads.

22/23. Work another row of lazy daisy rosebuds in pale pink, apricot or blue. Start four threads above and space alternatively to previous row.

24. French knots can be added to the tips of the buds of the last two pattern rows.

FRENCH KNOTS

Bring the needle up at A. Hold the thread firmly with the left thumb. Twist the needle once around the held thread.

Still holding the thread, turn the needle, with the twisted thread on it, and insert it into the material close to A and B. Do not relax the left thumb until the last minute. The knot should be pulled firmly.

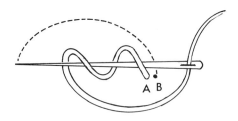

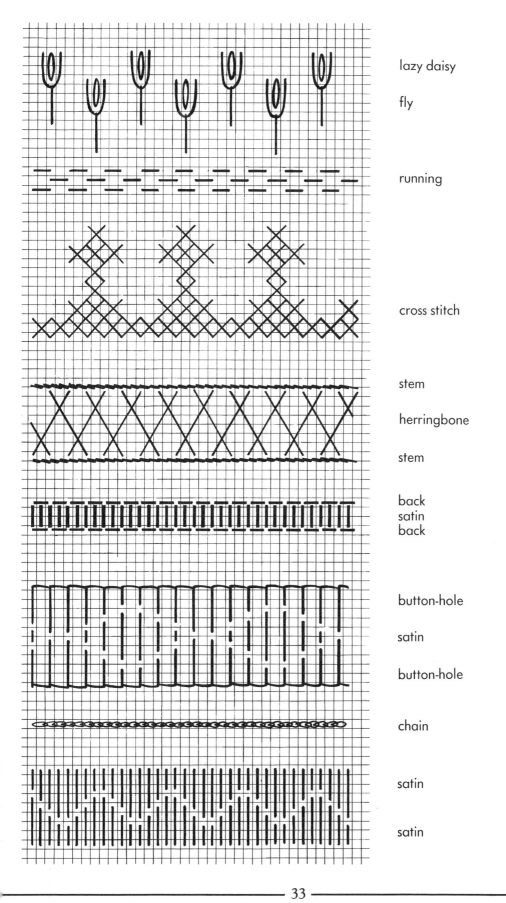

lazy daisy

fly

running

cross stitch

stem

herringbone

stem

back
satin
back

button-hole

satin

button-hole

chain

satin

satin

COLOUR CHART FOR MANY STITCHES BAG

Order of working	Colour
30 Lazy daisy stitch	palest pastel
29 Fly stitch	mid-green
28 Lazy daisy stitch	mid-pastel
27 Fly stitch	mid-green
26 Back stitch. Two rows	mid-pastel
25 Needle weaving	mid-pastel
24 French knots	yellow
23 Lazy daisy stitch	palest pastel
22 Button-hole stitch	mid-green
21 Chain stitch	mid-brown
20 Stem stitch	dark pastel
19 Fly stitch	pale green
18 Herringbone stitch	dark brown/mid-green/ darkest pastel
17 Back stitch 2	palest green
16 Back stitch	palest pastel/mid-brown
15 French knots	yellow
14 Lazy daisy	mid-pastel
13 Fly stitch	mid-green
12 Stem stitch	dark green
11 Satin stitch	dark pastel
10 Lazy daisy	yellow
9 Feather stitch	darkest brown
8 Satin stitch	mid-brown
7 Back stitch — done in 2 rows	mid-pastel
6 Button-hole stitch	mid-pastel
5 Button-hole stitch	mid-brown
4 Chain stitch	yellow
3 Stem stitch	mid-green
2 Satin stitch	dark pastel
1 Satin stitch (start on this line 6 cm (2½″) from bottom)	dark brown

TO MAKE THE BAG

Fold the material in half with the right side inside. Match the two ends of each row of embroidery carefully, pinning them together every 2 or 3 cm (¾″-1½″). Machine together. Complete the bag, securing the strap in the way you choose.

PIN CUSHION
FOR CHATELAINE

A chatelaine originally comprised a set of short chains attached to a woman's belt for carrying keys. The same principle can be applied to keep the essentials one needs for embroidery close to hand.

MATERIALS REQUIRED

- Even-weave linen, ecru, sufficient to cut out two circles of 8 cm (3″) diameter
- Two thin Dacron wadding circles, 5 cm (2″) in diameter
- Two circles of Pergasel, 5 cm (2″) in diameter
- Hand-made cord for trimming. See Project 19 for instructions
- DMC stranded cotton thread to match chatelaine
- Machine sewing cotton, ecru, to match linen
- Tapestry needle size 24
- Crewel needle size 6

METHOD

Count the threads in the linen circle, and tack across mid-line both ways. Follow the embroidery design in the chart. Start in centre with two strands of darker pink thread. Work the eight lazy daisy stitches, which form a square. With two strands of paler pink thread, embroider the three lazy daisy stitches for each point. Then the fly stitched stems are worked in one strand of green. Repeat for second side. Remove all tacking.

TO MAKE THE PIN CUSHION

Thread crewel needle with machine thread. Anchor the thread firmly about 1 cm (½″) from the edge of linen and sew with small running stitches around the whole circle. Leave needle attached. Put a circle of wadding onto the non-sticky side of the Pergasel circle. Place the embroidered circle carefully over the Dacron. Take

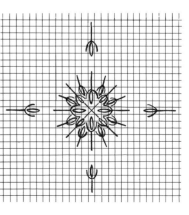

the paper off the Pergasel, revealing the sticky area. Draw up the thread sewn around the linen very firmly so that the linen is pulled firmly over the Dacron and the stiffening, and the embroidery is in the centre. Press the edges of the linen down onto the stiffening and finish by pulling needle and thread tightly. Hold in place with a back stitch. Repeat for second circle.

Put the two prepared circles together, with right sides out, and carefully sew them together so that they are even. A hand-made cord around the edge, with 12 cm (5″) ends to attach to chatelaine will complete the pin cushion. The pins are pushed in between the two circles, leaving the heads around the edge.

SCISSORS CASE
FOR CHATELAINE

MATERIALS REQUIRED

- Even-weave linen, ecru, 20 x 4 cm (8" x 2")
- Stiffening, Pergasel, 16 x 2 cm (6½" x 1"). (Plastic from lid of ice-cream container can be used)
- Hand-made cord for trimming. See Project 19 for instructions
- DMC stranded cotton thread to match chatelaine
- Machine sewing cotton No. 50, ecru, to match linen
- Tapestry needle size 24 or 26

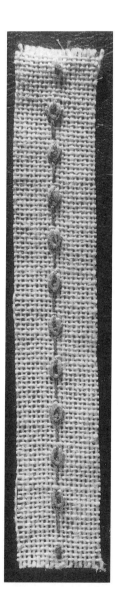

METHOD

Thread the needle with sewing-machine thread. Count threads to find the middle line down the length of the material. Tack down this line. Fold the two narrow ends together to determine the top and bottom of the scissor case. The fold is the bottom; tack across.

Begin rosebud embroidery six threads from the bottom. Thread needle with two strands of the darker pink thread. Embroider lazy daisy over three threads of the linen. Leave five threads and work another lazy daisy stitch. Continue towards the top of the case until only about 25 threads remain.

Thread the needle with two strands of pale pink thread and, using the same holes, work another lazy daisy stitch around the first.

The stalk is worked with one strand of green thread in fly stitch (see Project 3). Complete this side and repeat on second side.

TO MAKE THE SCISSORS CASE

Fold the stiffening in half and remove the paper backing. Stick the stiffening to the back of the linen, matching the tacking line at the bottom of the case with the fold in the stiffening. Make sure the linen is placed evenly down each side. Turn the sides of the linen in, over the stiffening. Turn the top of the case in. Pin both together carefully.

With machine thread, top sew down each side, beginning at the top. Sew over the top three stitches twice to strengthen. Complete scissors case by sewing a hand-made cord around three sides. Leave about 8 cm (3″) of cord at each side at the top to attach to the chatelaine.

THIMBLE BAG
FOR CHATELAINE

MATERIALS REQUIRED

- Even-weave linen, 12 x 6 cm (5″ x 2½″)
- Lining 12 x 6 cm (5″ x 2½″)
- Firm Vilene interlining, 12 x 6 cm (5″ x 2½″)
- DMC cotton perle thread No. 12, ecru
- Sewing-machine thread, ecru
- Needles and thread to match set
- Small button, such as a pearl bead, for securing bag
- Hand-made cord for attachment. See Project 19 for instructions

METHOD

Fold linen in half and tack across to mark the base of bag. Count 28 threads of linen from the base mark. With dark pink, begin the first row of rosebuds. Second rosebud is started three threads to the right and two threads up. Working to this count, make five buds. Now follow pattern by working four buds descending. This makes a pleasing zig-zag pattern.

Complete buds and stalks and two patterns ascending and descending to form the pattern. Repeat for the second side of the bag. Fold in sides of the bag, so that the embroidery almost meets at sides and tack down. The two narrow ends of the material form the top of the bag. These are worked in nun's stitch using cotton perle No. 12.

NUN'S STITCH

Start with a tail. Bring the needle up on the line to be cut off 1 cm (½″) from edge A. If the cutting line is held to the left, put the needle in over two threads to the right at B. Bring the needle up again at A. Repeat once. Bring the needle up two threads down at C. Put the needle in again at B, bring the needle up at D two threads to the left of C. Continue in this way across each end of the material.

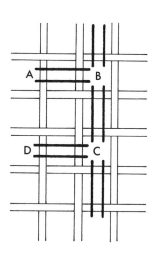

Lay this linen piece flat and measure carefully. It should measure about 10 x 4 cm (4" x 1½"), so cut out a piece of Vilene 5 mm (¼") smaller each way. Use a set-square to be exact. With the tacking thread, sew the lining onto the Vilene, turning over the edges exactly, as in patchwork. Place this on the linen and pin carefully and evenly.

Using machine sewing thread, sew all around without letting any stitches show on the right side of the linen. Remove tacking. Pin the two sides of the bag together, matching the tops of the embroidery. Top sew edges together, making the top edge very secure and neat.

BUTTON AND LOOP CLOSURE

Find the middle of the front edge of the little bag, and mark with pins 2 mm (⅕") each side of this middle line, on the edge. Thread the needle with machine cotton. Put the needle in between the thickness of material about 2 cm (1") away from the pins. Bring the needle up at the first pin, right on the edge A. Put the needle in at the second pin B and take it out at A, sliding it inside the thicknesses of material. The thread between A and B forms the loop which must be big enough for the button to pass through. Make three more loops the same size into the same two holes.

EDGE OF
MATERIAL   A - - - - - B

Starting at A and working from left to right, work in button-hole stitch over these four threads. Pull the thread firmly and do as many stitches as will make a firm, tidy loop. Run the needle through the thicknesses of materials about 2 cm (1"). Cut off excess thread.

A cream pearl bead makes an attractive small button. Sew it on securely with machine thread to the edge. The thimble case is now ready to attach to the chatelaine by a hand-made cord. Sew this along three sides and leave about 8 cm (3") on each end.

NEEDLE CASE
FOR CHATELAINE

MATERIALS REQUIRED

- Even-weave linen, ecru, 6 x 8 cm (2½″ x 3″)
- Lining — piece of thin cotton patterned material 6 x 8 cm (2½″ x 3″)
- Thick Vilene 6 x 4 cm (2½″ x 1½″)
- Small piece of Dacron wadding approximately 5 x 2 cm (2″ x 1″)
- Cream flannel 6 x 4 cm (2½″ x 1½″)
- Threads to match chatelaine
- DMC cotton perle thread, ecru, No. 12
- Sewing-machine thread, ecru
- Tapestry needle size 24 or 26 for embroidery
- Crewel needle size 10 for sewing case together
- Hand-made cord, 24 cm (9½″). See Project 19 for instructions
- Small button, such as a pearl bead

METHOD

Fold the linen in half. Mark fold line with a pin. Thread the needle with the machine thread and tack along the line marked. Fold the linen in half the opposite way. Mark fold line with a pin and tack along the line marked. Count 12 threads in (from beside the tacking thread) on one of the long sides. Mark with a pin. Start here.

Thread the needle with DMC cotton perle. Begin with a tail. Embroider in satin stitch over two threads until you have worked 38 stitches. Turn the linen and bring the needle up into the hole nearest to centre of linen of the last stitch. Continue in satin stitch until you have completed 46 stitches. Turn the corner as before. Work 76 satin stitches along the third side. Turn as before. Work 46 satin stitches along this side. Turn and complete the first side. Finish in the usual way.

Thread the needle with two strands of green thread. Count six threads from the tacking line of a long side

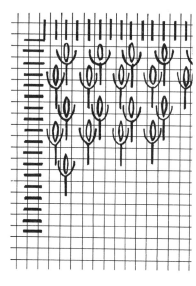

and three threads inside satin-stitched border. Embroider in satin stitch over two threads.

When you have worked 28 stitches and five threads remain, turn by bringing the needle back into the top hole of the last stitch. Continue for 37 stitches (five threads away from the border). Turn as before and work 28 stitches before turning. Turn and complete the fourth side.

The lazy daisy as a filling stitch is embroidered with a single lazy daisy stitch, and a fly stitch stalk. You will see by the picture where to put the stitches. The back of the needle-case book has the same cross-stitch border as the chatelaine strap, but is worked over two threads of the linen. Count as you did for the green satin stitch on the border on the front.

If you wish to put your initials on this, embroider them in one strand of dark pink, working them in back stitch from your chart.

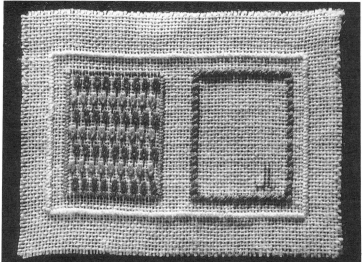

TO ASSEMBLE

Turn the embroidered linen in all around, leaving the satin stitch showing. This leaves a space of single linen thickness in the middle. Cut a piece of Dacron wadding to fill this space. Tack in place. Cut the Vilene 2 mm (1/5″) smaller than the satin-stitch edge of the linen. Use a set-square to ensure exact corners.

Using the Vilene as a template, turn the lining over the edge as if for patchwork. Tack neatly in place. Put the prepared lining onto the wrong side of the linen. Pin evenly in place and, with very tiny stitches, sew in place, leaving the Vilene sandwiched between. If you have been exact in the measurements, the lining will sit inside the line with a 1 mm (1/10″) space evenly all around.

Cut the cream flannel the same size as the lining, using the set-square for accuracy. Fold the flannel, and the linen book cover in half (like a book) and press. Open the flannel and place on top of the opened book cover. The two fold lines must now be put together evenly and pinned in place.

Thread the needle with machine thread and sew the flannel to the needle case. Sew through all materials. A piece of hand-made cord 24 cm (9½″) long will be needed to attach the needle case to the chatelaine. Fold the cord in half. Put the end of the loop to the bottom of the needle case. One half of the cord goes along the outside and the other half along the inside of the case. Very small, neat stitches hold it in place on the inside. Sew the two pieces of cord together at the top of the case.

A button and a loop will keep the needle case closed. Find the middle of the front edge of the little book, mark with pins 2 mm (⅕″) each side of this middle line, on the edge. Thread the needle with sewing machine cotton. Put the needle in between the thickness of material about 2 cm (1″) away from the pins. Bring the needle up at the first pin right on the edge A. Put the needle in at the second pin B and take it out at A, sliding it inside the thickness of material. The thread between A and B forms the loop, which must be big enough for the button to pass through.

Make three more loops the same size into the same two holes. Starting at A and working from left to right, work in button-hole stitch over these four threads. Pull the thread firmly and do as many stitches as will make a firm, tidy loop. Run the needle through the thicknesses of materials about 2 cm (1″). Cut off excess thread.

A cream pearl bead makes an attractive small button. Sew it on securely with machine thread to the edge.

STRAP FOR CHATELAINE

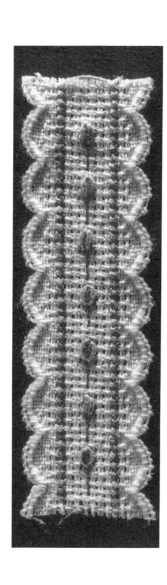

MATERIALS REQUIRED

- 1 metre (39″) of commercial braid (even-weave), ecru, approximately 2.5 cm (1″) wide
- DMC stranded cotton thread, green 502, pink 899, pink 309
- Tapestry needle size 24 or 26
- Hand-made cord. See instructions below

METHOD

Thread the needle with two strands of green thread. Embroider a row of alternate green and pink cross stitches along each side of the braid. See photograph. You may like to embroider your name along the chatelaine. Find the middle of the strap and embroider your name and age and the year in which you are making the chatelaine. Work from the chart, in back stitch, as in Project 3, over one square of the material. The rosebuds embroidered on the rosebud bag are the ones used for this project. This time, they will follow the line of the braid, leaving four clear squares between. If they are embroidered with the stalks pointing to the ends of the strap, they will look good when the strap is hung around the neck.

HAND-MADE CORD

Take two lengths of stranded thread (all six strands in each). If you need 20 cm (8″) of cord you will need three times 20 cm plus about 10 cm (4″). So, you need two lengths of thread 70 cm (28″) long. Knot them together close to each end. Put a pencil at each end between the two threads. You need a friend to take one end while you take the other end. You must stand far enough away from each other to keep the threads taut. Hold the threads together between your finger and thumb, close to the pencil. Twist the pencil, like a propeller, away from you. Your friend does the same. Keep twisting until the cord begins to 'kink'. Then, still keeping the threads taut, use your other hand to bring the two ends together. When the twisted threads are folded in half evenly, let the folded end go. *Knot the other ends together or they will untwist.* You can now help it to twist together a little more. The cords you make will be tighter (better) if you make short lengths.

TO ATTACH THE TOOLS TO THE CHATELAINE STRAP

Arrange to have one tool of similar weight or bulk on each end plus one of the less bulky ones. Knot the two ends of each tool case together with a reef knot. Trim the ends. Place two of these knotted loops across the wrong side of one end of the embroidered strap. Fold the end of the strap over, about 1 cm (½″). Then make a second fold over the cords. Make this fold as tidy and neat as you can, and pin it in place.

Thread the needle with sewing-machine thread and with neat, small, almost invisible stitches fasten it in place. Treat the other end in the same way. Many embroiderers enjoy wearing a chatelaine when they are sewing, to keep essential items to hand.

WHITE LINEN MAT

So many people today use even-weave fabrics and counted-thread embroidery techniques that it seemed fitting to promote the technique of white work in this book, with this small, simple example. A handkerchief could be made in the same way, using a piece of linen approximately 30 cm (10″) square.

MATERIALS REQUIRED

- Linen sheeting (not an even-weave fabric) 15 x 15 cm (6″ x 6″). Handkerchief linen may be used but it is more flimsy
- DMC stranded cotton thread, white
- Machine sewing cotton 50, white
- Crewel needles sizes 10 and 12

METHOD

Draw out two threads (one at a time) from the material, 3 cm (1″) from the edge. Leave five threads of the fabric. Draw out two more threads from the inner side of the already drawn threads. Repeat this on all sides. Thread the size 10 needle with machine thread. Hemstitch around mat on the innermost edge of drawn threads.

BUTTON-HOLE STITCHING

Thread the size 10 needle with two strands of thread. Embroider in button-hole stitch. Start with running stitch, to anchor thread. Bring the needle up (not at a corner) into the outer row of drawn threads. Work over the five threads left for the purpose. The stitches must be sewn very closely together and pulled firmly.

At the corner, take the needle down into the one central hole while bringing the thread up evenly around the edge. Complete all four sides. When all the embroidery has been completed, carefully trim the edge of the linen, close to the button-hole stitch.

TO DECORATE

Trace the small design of flowers and bow onto one corner of the mat. Thread the size 12 needle with one strand of thread. The flowers are worked in whipped back stitch, 1 mm (1/10") each. The leaves are worked in chain stitch, 1 mm (1/10"). The centre of each flower is an eyelet. The bow is outlined in stem stitch. Succeeding rows of stem stitch are worked very closely to the preceding row until the whole shape is filled.

WHIPPED BACK STITCH

Embroider the design in back stitch, then put the needle under each stitch — but not into the material. Pull firmly.

EYELETS

Thread the needle with one strand of thread. Put a large, thick needle into the material on the dot in the centre of the flower. Move it around stretching the linen in order to make a definite hole. Sew around the hole with very small stitches as close to the edge as possible. Continue with the same thread, top sewing closely all around, and pulling the thread firmly. This will form a cord-like edge. Fasten off in usual way.

BIBLIOGRAPHY

Anchor Manual of Needlework, J & P Coats Ltd, Batsford, London.

Encyclopedia of Needlework, Thérèse de Dillmont, DMC Library.

Mary Thomas's Dictionary of Embroidery Stitches, Hodder & Stoughton.

Weldon's Encyclopedia of Needlework, The Waverley Book Co.